Tenderness

THE ISABELLA GARDNER POETRY AWARD FOR 2021

TENDERNESS

POEMS BY

DERRICK AUSTIN

AMERICAN POETS CONTINUUM SERIES, NO. 187

BOA EDITIONS, LTD. ❦ ROCHESTER, NY ❦ 2021

First Edition
21 22 23 24 7 6 5 4 3 2 1

For information about permission to reuse any material from this book, please contact
The Permissions Company at www.permissionscompany.com or e-mail permdude@
gmail.com.

Publications by BOA Editions, Ltd.—a not-for-profit corporation
under section 501 (c) (3) of the United States Internal Revenue
Code—are made possible with funds from a variety of sources,
including public funds from the Literature Program of the National
Endowment for the Arts; the New York State Council on the Arts, a
state agency; and the County of Monroe, NY. Private funding sources
include the Max and Marian Farash Charitable Foundation; the
Mary S. Mulligan Charitable Trust; the Rochester Area Community
Foundation; the Ames-Amzalak Memorial Trust in memory of Henry
Ames, Semon Amzalak, and Dan Amzalak; the LGBT Fund of Greater Rochester;
and contributions from many individuals nationwide. See Colophon on page 84 for
special individual acknowledgments.

Cover Design: Sandy Knight
Cover Art: *blessed are the mosquitos* by Diedrick Brackens
Interior Design and Composition: Richard Foerster
BOA Logo: Mirko

BOA Editions books are available electronically through BookShare, an online dis-
tributor offering Large-Print, Braille, Multimedia Audio Book, and Dyslexic formats,
as well as through e-readers that feature text to speech capabilities.

Library of Congress Cataloging-in-Publication Data
Names: Austin, Derrick, 1989- author.
Title: Tenderness / Derrick Austin.
Description: First edition. | Rochester, NY : BOA Editions, Ltd., 2021. |
  Series: American poets continuum series ; no. 187 | "The Isabella
  Gardner Poetry Award for 2021"
Identifiers: LCCN 2021012432 (print) | LCCN 2021012433 (ebook) | ISBN
  9781950774395 (paperback) | ISBN 9781950774401 (ebook)
Subjects: LCGFT: Poetry.
Classification: LCC PS3601.U857 T46 2021 (print) | LCC PS3601.U857
  (ebook) | DDC 811/.6—dc23
LC record available at https://lccn.loc.gov/2021012432
LC ebook record available at https://lccn.loc.gov/2021012433

BOA Editions, Ltd.
250 North Goodman Street, Suite 306
Rochester, NY 14607
www.boaeditions.org
A. Poulin, Jr., Founder (1938–1996)

for Cody, Lauren, and Marcelo

All through my boyhood I was told I'd walk hand in hand
with death. I chose the good, and cried
when they marred the statues.
But there is nothing, nothing to say about my life.

—Linda Gregg

Contents

Days of 2014

He had told me to circle the lake.
Smell of pepper and pine resin.
Black people died or went missing
that summer, everyday it seemed,
and here was someone who wanted to find me.
We drank red wine, heavy and bitter.
Sunlight moved across the lake with the hours;
terns mixed their shadows and bodies in the water.
When he laughed, a little foam
gathered on his incisors. He helped me into the wild grass
and slash pines when I couldn't walk.
There is a roof one man's body makes over another.
Pine needles on sharp grains. This is what I remember.
This is how I escaped the world. A little foam.

Tenderness

That summer I was a body. I was that body. The Body.
Overnight, a fog of linen inside the mauve Victorian down the block.
Another house empty for the season, for the season, for the season.
Hours built up on both sides of my bedroom door.
Morgan and Danez rowed in the Grand Canal at Versailles.
Morgan filled a postcard with her hands and memory.
Rose quartz? A diary? Holy water? (With what belief?) What could I
    have asked for?
Leaving my apartment for the first time in days,
I walked five minutes to Lake Mendota. Barking, honking, shrieking,
    grunting.
Men tested their bodies for each other and themselves.
Opened doors to admit the breeze, the possibility of that one guest.
When Emily Brontë wrote *they've gone through and through me, like*
    wine through water,
and altered the colour of my mind, she wasn't writing about my depression.
Double tapped a photo of Morgan and Angel
posing near a green door with hinges older than the Constitution.
They read their black poems in English
to black people who spoke English and French and Arabic.
If I sent a postcard to everyone I loved
it'd say, *Sometimes I think you're just too good for me.*
The most personal question I'm consistently asked: *Why are you so quiet?*
That I'm getting this all down wrong. That I'm getting it down at all.

Is This or Is This True as Happiness

When we finally make it, we sit on cold stones.
The river curling over and under our feet
even colder. His secret place.

The air has that early fall smell, things beginning
to rot, the wet soil nourishing itself.
We're trespassing.

Anything could happen
to me in this white ass town. I'm terrified
if he knows that and terrified if he doesn't.

My body is puffy, unremarkable.
I've grown distant and sullen.
A witch told me gin placates the dead.

Whose dead have I been trying to drown
drinking my own elegy?
He asks if I'm happy, and I say yes. *See how easy it is*

to get here, he says. *Yes,*
I say. *But you have to take me back.*

Twitter Break: I Watch a Movie

Jackie (dir. Pablo Larraín)

There's a scene where the First Lady is possessed by the opera of her life. It's late evening, probably midnight. "Camelot" blares through The White House. Her comportment sustains a lyric fugue. In every room she enters there is a luxe familiar texture. She tries on pearls. She drinks a glass of red. She tries on a blue gown. She drinks vodka. To take some control of her life, she allows herself to become an image for her country, a country that adores the image of a grieving woman.

Images of black pain are liked and shared.
America would make icons of black women
and have them in their best black every day.

Dorian Corey

"The Drag Queen Had a Mummy In Her Closet"
—*New York Magazine*, 1995

I shot him, but everyone deserves a house
to be remembered in. I locked him in my trunk
of rhinestones, crowns, and sable stoles.
He tried to rob me. Read the magazines.

Mother in my mother's house at eight,
I diapered my half-brother and tested milk,
a brief, pearl bracelet on my wrist.
I dropped my name years later, and, reborn,
mothered myself and many more—without
a house to keep us, we're good as dead.

Read the news. Listen. A girl, I knew,
femme realness to a T, Evangelista on a magazine,
Venus Xtravaganza turned it out.
God knows the doll was fierce. She wanted love
and cash, of course. She followed johns
into their limousines. Room service found her

under a bed: some trick strangled Venus.
It took four days for someone to claim her.
I'm sick of sequin veils and mourning gowns.
I'm sick of empty brownstones, these dark homes.

The Witching Hour

C'mon, pour another, my mother's friend says.
The juke throbs.
                    Everybody black dancing The Wobble
in that Florida town. Tonic fizzes in two fingers of vodka.
As my mother
                    commemorates her beauty with a selfie,
I dance with trees

that are not trees but black and brown people. Strobe lights
flower on our arms.

The only gay bar in this Midwestern town is Live,
not as in *give* but
                    hive—imagine if bees were nocturnal,
making physical what night is
on their patrols: possibility. Imagine centuries of women
                              walking alone in the woods
(burned), living foreign and old (jailed), naming
names (_____).
                    The femme queen grinding against me
         grants me passage
into a pleasure at once hers and only mine and ours.

Who we are to each other on the dance floor shifts,
a friend an hour, then no one.
                              I will always be
my mother's child. Even now she keeps me in attention
in the great night of her mind:
worry and hope and the skulking moon over hazy water.

Tomorrow she will text to make sure I'm alive.

Late Summer

Strobe lights swarmed over the dead in Orlando.
A cop executed Philando Castile in front of his beloved and her daughter.
Citizens shared the video on their timelines.
I cloistered myself in grief. I didn't shave.
Mom said I looked like a wildcat. Was I an I?

A man I'd been fucking took me sailing on Lake Mendota.
We heard the disordered drums and yelps
Of a woman who shouldn't sing marimba music
From the crescent of light where people caroused and forgot themselves.
He returned me to simplicity, lust, selfishness
—Of the powers that separate us from animals, cruelty.
He kissed me and groped between my legs.
I stopped desiring him months ago.
My pleasure was in his not knowing and wanting me still.

Proverb

Terror infests the heart like hornets
which breed in a miasma of violence,
whose brood vomit a sugar substance
      for the nest—
        no room for a friend.

Flies

I waste the morning in bed eating Talenti and chocolate-
covered almonds infused with cannabis.

The only people I've talked to in weeks are the father
and son who own the corner store.

The father blocked me on a meat market of an app.
My ego compulsively licks its wounds.

Your type, a friend texts me, is the kind of man
Lee Pace could play in his sleep: cerebral, imperious.

Books cover the other half of my bed.
In the one I've nearly finished, a prince becomes a hermit,

his soul growing receptive and active
like a plant consuming green flies.

Thinking of Romanticism, Thinking of Drake

You rake! You're Lord Byron burning off
Hennessy and pound cake in Lake Geneva—
oh, but how your sunbright body slakes my thirst.

And though it's another record-breaking fall,
weeks of extravagant sunlight wilt the gentians,
the sunflowers, sick of it, droop and go bald,

the geese fly south, volley after volley
over Villa Diodati, to preen and rest on the lake.
They were fuckboys of a revolutionary age—

not the geese, Byron and Shelley—the old regimes,
unable to get away with violence casually, revised
and carried on business as usual in the summer of 1816

when there was no summer, only rain and chills.
Thunder quaked the triplet windows in the villa
where they wrote about their time and the dead.

The dead waste no time telling the story of our age.
Their refusal is not new, only louder now like sunlight.
Nationalism is not new, only louder now like sunlight.

Uninsured. Self-medicating. Distracting myself,
I photoshopped you into *Wanderer above the Sea of Fog,*
above the Statue of Liberty and Michael Jordan's weeping dome.

How is it where you are? Up there. In your feelings.
In your body, your beautiful, breathing body.

To Friendship

After a stress dream, I hallucinated a large, hairy spider on the wall.

More and more lately, I wake up to a hairy spider.

I close my eyes and a weight presses on my chest.

I drink Prosecco from a paper cup.

From the futon, my view is a stand of pine trees and the luminous lake.

My friends sleep in other rooms.

We pooled our money for a weekend cabin.

We breathe together.

On our trip, we ask for what we need without fear;

we refill each other's cups—

I didn't know I could choose any of this.

Letter to Brandon

I wish you were with me when I saw
the most stylish black woman stroll down State Street
in a red velvet coat. It was like a scene out of *The Hours*.
Carrying a bouquet, she entered those apartments
near our favorite Italian place
(remember our muscular waiter's gentle voice?).
Her lilies—for her bae, I hoped—brightened an afternoon
of two women detangling hair.
Is this how you write fiction? Plot isn't fate exactly.
Drinking rosé at Gib's, I thought of you typing
in your dream house near Canada,
the shadows of spruces on a lake. I'd be somewhere else,
who knows where, waiting for your stories
where no choice is barred or above consideration.

Birth Chart

Back home where the Gulf is historian
and time, it's hurricane season:
don't think I make light of water

barreling into homes, cane fields laid low—
it began like this for me you know,
rocking in the undertow of my mother,

sustained by what is flowing and free,
still able to breathe that water.

I was born in south Florida.
Storms were named. My father named me.
Charts for potential and charts for disaster.

I was one of many black children alive in America.
Hurricane Hugo ravaged the Antilles.
The sun was in Virgo and the moon in Cancer.

My Education

I didn't know what they were talking about
at the table with their glasses of bitter red.
Even their laughter didn't belong to them.
The affected way they moved their hands
like stage actors from another century.
My parents were teaching me about love or money.
A peevish child, I had not found my intelligence.
My body, my emotions, and my eyes were separate.
Play rough. Draw blood. Don't speak. No tears.
Hardening. Boys hardening. Hardening in my underwear.
Often I imagined myself as a glamorous white woman
in a sequin gown, hat tilted just so.
I laugh at it now. A laugh cry. Oh to be
any kind of dress. Any kind of event in it.

Any kind of dress, any kind of event in it,
I laugh at it now. A laugh cry. Oh to be
in a sequin gown, hat tilted just so.
Often I imagined myself as a glamorous white woman.
Hardening. Boys hardening. Hardening in my underwear.
Play rough. Draw blood. Don't speak. No. Tears.
My body, my emotions, and my eyes were separate.
A peevish child, I had not found my intelligence.
My parents were teaching me about love or money
like stage actors from another century:
the affected way they moved their hands,
even their laughter didn't belong to them
at the table with their glasses of bitter red.
I didn't know what they were talking about.

Now that I've survived when does living begin?

Little Epic

The capital is already underwater, the inside
of a sea god's throat or, maybe, his liver.
There's a boy in a rowboat. The only
survivor, let's say. Moonlight, stars, a good wind.
Black Aeneas without a father on his back.
Already the boy is a failure. His name
is Lyric. Emancipation unsettles him.
Who said liberty was a field of lavender
studded with bees? Who said it wasn't a sea?
Risk and Refusal, these will be the twins
that guide toward no empire.
Let there be a kind of Carthage for the boy,
illuminated by fires not of grief or betrayal,
rough harbor where he will be a man unbecoming.

Epithalamium

Today I'm happy by myself
wandering this creek's paths of sand and crushed shells,
        what used to be submerged.

Mosquitos drain me good.

Before this river was redirected, it joined two others
        and flowed into the Gulf.

What we cannot change, we evade
        and call new. We delay. I could
call the irrigation works at the headwater bog
                an aubade
        against flooding.

There are picnic spots nearby, gazebos and grills
emerging from palmettos and bindweed.
A storm blew down the oak I'd climb to watch
fireworks for free.

Men still cruise out here.

In this lush expanse a man
was lynched
at the beginning of the century
I was born in.

Moving off the trail, I wade into the river.
Time feels suspended.
My bare feet
shuffle pebbles like some grubbing shore bird.

Screeching insects, thickets of sweet bay and titi,
moldering scent—

All this will be gone someday.
Gone the paths and signs, gone the milkweed, gone
the armadillos and the field
and the lynching tree when this river rejoins the others
and washes this away—
                              no, not gone
but come together, history, nature, love, and loss
brought to scale in a glorious
algal bloom, a brightness of jade and amber,
all this water moving toward where it's always belonged,
where I cannot be, where I am.

The Devil's Book

There's no fun in witchery these days.
Sure, I shudder cops with invisible needles,
but magic's no calling. I simply asked to die

on my own terms.
Meanwhile, the Earth's sick
of our ego. It will outlast us. We'll burn

ourselves out and no one will grieve
and good riddance—

Devil take us.

Tituba refused The Devil's Book. Before the good people,
she testified: *I love the dust on my heels when I am luxurious*

alone
and they heard dancing with the Devil.
God gave me imagination and a just will
and they heard the flight of women

above the steeple and meeting house.
Tituba was no witch. She simply saw the nooses
each citizen held.

They ran themselves ragged.

Hotline Bling (Voicemail)

Ever since I left the city, you got me fucked up. Can't even say, D____.
Your name inked on the sweetmeat of my thigh, crossed out: ~~Drake~~.

What happens to a meme deferred? Does he thirst trap on Instagram?
Sip D'Ussé with Odell? I loved you before the beard and protein shakes.

Morgan says: *We should all get free therapy. We could call it reparations.*
Can I dance inside a SAD lamp? My feelings are obsidian, opaque.

Two things don't abandon black people: death and style. And death
Learned living from us. Derivative and late, it whines. It bellyaches.

                        Calling you was my first mistake, Aubrey.
I masturbate. I dream you do not move but grant for prayers' sake.

I dream that you and I don't move. What gives the night its name?
What bloody sway? Like a mandrake, I holler (D____!) when I wake.

Black Docent

after Darren Waterston's "Filthy Lucre"

In 1877, Whistler painted *The Peacock Room* for a patron
he grew to hate: fights over integrity and money
inspired his harmony of blue and green.
Waterston makes this drama explicit by imagining that room
ravaged by time. These sensuous peacocks in heat—
one snatches the entrails from another's throat.
I recognize these peacock-men.
They never know what room they're in
even when I'm there. They don't feel guilty
when they're done with me.
Whistler painted *The Peacock Room*
140 years ago. Slavery had not been excised
from the Americas. I've wanted
to be hurt into gold.

Villiers

What's patience to the affection of a king?
I always hated that verse about the meek.

One gesture splintered into—kisses, antique
glass—a cosmos of goodness. The house

where we were husbands was ornamental.
We drank chocolate, sometimes port.

I ignored my wedding vows and you the state.
What's more erotic than the dream of control?

Honeysuckles you swallowed, I swallowed.
Sunset was pollen blown off your shoulder.

Translators made new music from Hebrew.
During your reign, witches burned.

—In your bedroom, which echoed our more
extravagant positions, did you read my love letter?

Black Dandy

Under the shaggy honeysuckle, its sweet bruised heat,
its migraine of scent, I remember
the first time I tasted a flower: playing with the other kids,
we beset whole shrubs
with our sticky silly hands. We pretended
to be knights, carried a stolen cabbage we called Old Pilgrim,
and took turns holding the head
until it fell apart. Even though it rained that morning,
the sky was bright and the air
humid in the shade of trees we played under.
When one of the boys scraped himself, I'd split dandelions
and rub the milky halves into the cuts on his knee.
I often didn't look them in the eyes, jealous
of their eagerness to rejoin the others and climb a new branch.
In my bedroom that night, listening to Phyllis Hyman,
I admired my quartz collection.
I finish my slurry of gin and ice.
The pills that rescue my mind make sleep difficult.
Palm trees like glaives. Wind from the east. Overhead,
white and yellow flowers shift one way, another if I turn my face.

Dear & Decorations

I ought to see myself as a man. Be proud and grateful.
I'd rather be your ermine with a silver bell
on my pink satin collar. Let my farewell and arrival
tease the same gasp from you. Let your sound
surprise you every time. If you grant a silk pillow,
I'll make of myself a moon your guests can admire.
When lords throw bloody chunks at their hounds,
impress them with your finger dipped in honey or olive oil,
all I need to survive. Let saints be wrapped in swaddling
clothes: cradle me, I'll warm your hands. Tonight,
there is a fire, carafes of wine, silver dishes of sweets
and almonds. You recite a French fairy tale called "Winter"
while the shadows of snowflakes drift across the floor.
It's the climax of a story about exile, which is a love story, too.
The prince is scarred, has grown a grief-beard. He's slain
the scaled beast, its eyes bright as a fallen star, its back
like a nautilus. He's assumed the position of Christ.
Three times, he's spurned the love of the Fairy Queen.
Until now he's refused to ask for help or protection.
I would be too ashamed to ask for these were I a man.
The sky in the tale is like the sky outside: pinkish-gray,
a greenhouse of jasmine and lilac filled with smoke.
When the prince trudges out of the cold, tall as the pines,
hair crowned with white that melts and chills again
on his neck and ears, and rests his head on his lord's lap,
breaking the curse, your ladies draw closer to each other,
their silences nearly touching. They return to their chambers
when the story ends. You put me in a cage and go to bed.
The fireplace bares red fangs. Outside, the fox and bear.
The last of the hunters return home with their kills,
rabbits and squirrels they'll skin and dress. They are silent.
Bulky in fur, they are some new creature, a little blood

staining here and there. Who is not with them? What loss
will harden their hearts because they won't speak of it?
Would they know how? They are changed. They are at the gates.

Remembering God After Three Years of Depression

Where were your rough, familiar hands
smelling of rosemary? Insomnia watched me,
wild-haired and unwashed, like an officer.
Perhaps the light through the keyhole
was you, floorboards straining in another room.
In the hall, a sleepwalker sang the blues,
bleeding dream into the world.
I feared a knock at the door. I needed a hand.
Would you have found me on the deflated air
mattress, among filthy shirts, half-eaten food?
I don't know what to call doubt when you are here
and I am not. What is it to be exiled in you?
Maybe if I'd been drinking red instead of white.
I had no space in me for less than life.

Let Them Be Not What They Were Made For

There are two men inside me, and they're not speaking. Well,
       one's dead—his corpse hardens in snow. Snow
in his open mouth. The other stinks of wet dogs and iron.
       The landscape is what would unfashionably be called my soul.
The landscape, were it a painting, would be called *Forbidden Princess*.
       They've been at this for years. I don't want moans or broken
promises anymore. Enough white-knuckling. Wilgefortis,
       with your strong arms like Christ, with your milk and wonder
like Christ, bring heaven down, briefly, sweetly now, where
       there are words for everything. A heaven wider than androgyny
is sugar on my tongue. Of the dead man, who will claim him?
       Was he ever a man? He's not unlike a tree now. If I can imagine
my own blossoms, listen for my rightful name and say it, then
       spring? Of the living man—the opposite of winter is the sea.

Cachet & Compassion

We kiss in parting and greeting. Brother John painted our Black Madonna and close as he was to her face, he often preaches, he was never closer to wisdom. Brother Benjamin, difficult at times, but full of rue and regret that he cannot control his need to order—utensils, stones, usually books—taps himself wildly and sometimes wails. Brother Baptiste once asked, *How do I fit into my body?* Brother Javier survived the plague. We think nothing of his fever-whitened hair: no one returns untouched from death's strange land. Brother Jeremiah covers pears in cloth to protect from sudden frost. We've only read about the sea, but after a day's labor he smelled like my dream of the sea. Sometimes, my Brother offers a pear and knife, its handle made lustrous through the passing of hands.

Letter to Cody on Walpurgisnacht

Again last night I dreamed the dream called Femme:
in it, my rings and Jungle Red nails flickered against my caftan;
I wrapped my hair in white, after my great-grandmother,
and walked down the street without incident in ordinary air.
Shame comes from the phrase *to cover,* did you know?
Cackling over whiskey, I wasn't afraid for both of us.
We could live deliciously. You said my gender was glamour,
and I believed you. In another version of our lives we were sisters
trundling up the Brocken to meet the coven, bramble and thistle
whispering underfoot. On the mountaintop, there was no
great-horned gentleman in black, no babies boiling in fat.
Why are we only remembered covered in blood and gristle?
Whirling around a fire, we were allowed, briefly, our bodies,
far from the burnings in Würzburg, Bamberg, and Trier.

Sadness Isn't the Only Muse

I can't imagine myself reading bedtime stories
to a toddler, and I'm older than my father was
when he read those brightly colored books to me.
His voice is deeper than mine will ever be
but just as sweet. I always picked *Freight Train*.
I loved the black caboose. *A train runs across this track . . .*
through tunnels and cities, darkness and light, forever.
I still love books where nothing happens,
good or bad. The page is one landscape I move through.

Son Jarocho

for Marcelo, Rubi, and JD

1. Cocktails at the Palacio de Bellas Artes

except for the bartender this space is all yours.
anonymous in your blackness,
safe with friends, be especially fey.

order your drink. stumble through Spanish.
in murals above: marching workers,
an indigenous man face down on a slab,

flogging and gore, shackles and guns—
don't make a fetish of suffering. sip your drink.
when Marcelo asks what you'll remember

mention the mountains and delicious food.
when he says *I've never seen such poverty*, drink again.
shame as tonic with your glass of mostly gin.

history is an awful flirt.
their chapels and art, tired pick-up lines,
seduce you worst of all.

are you less sore? are you too hot?
watch for rain. watch the police with their riot gear.
order another round. tip as much as you can.

2. Mexico City Metropolitan Cathedral

Despite the cathedral's vaulted roof,
the Altar of Forgiveness
bright with imperial gold, it was hard to see.

What little light there was
had the quality of stone.
Paintings barred to me by shadows, rails.

I knew these images of grief by heart,
mother and son, brutality and love,
cyclical as a soap opera.

I tried remaining aloof to those praying,
leaving bouquets at the altar.
Women on their knees, like the men.

I wished I could touch the brown Christ,
read the psalter.
I was looking for an antidote

to Europe and America.
When we entered,
Rubi dipped her hand in water and crossed herself.

3. Teotihuacán

Not even the gods would have begrudged us
        that view. Perched on the Temple of the Moon,

Rubi took our picture,
        none of us particularly out of place,
black or brown and thankful
        to be there.

We saw why the gods
dwelled where stone leopards and serpents
refuse to become dust:

        vistas broad and old
as the first uttered sound. To think of it
        still makes me sweat.
We descended with three Mexican women.
        I gripped the lone cord,
        terrified of stairs
not cut for my clown feet. They chatted
with JD and I though, shamefully, we couldn't communicate.

They wanted a picture
under a wind-ruined shrine.
Smiling, we linked arms.

4. *Obsidian Mirror*

Don't take anything from Teotihuacán, JD.
          Watch it be cursed. I gotta fly back with your ass!
The man who sold it was sweet,
          and it was a gorgeous, polished stone.
Night entered the mirror and brightened
          where we saw our unburdened faces.

We were black men in a city,
          an oasis, where we need not
flinch at another's approach.
          This city never was ours.
On the train ride back, I saw a politician
          on the front page, recently elected,
bloody and strung-up. We walked avenues
          where the poor with open palms called me *moreno*.
On hookup apps, men cursed our English advances.

5. *Adult Film Festival*

Avoiding rain, we dipped inside a church
where whites with locs, all matted up in knots,
watched German women shouting at their subs
barking in latex shorts and canine masks.
We listened to Teutonic syllables
ricochet off columns and reach the dome
wine-dark with haughty cherubim at rest
while Peter guards another kind of bliss.
A perfect kind of sacrilege, I thought,
this global festival of sex, delight
in porn that's nothing less than Genesis
uncut, no shame-inducing fruit; humans
made fluid, out of dew and rain, not dust,
mask for mask no more, and vulnerable.

6. Casa Azul

Marcelo left his iPhone in a taxi, so we lost our photos of Frida Kahlo's house. Still, I can't forget seeing her easel and dried paints. *Marcelo,* said Frida's death mask. He touched the shawl wrapped with flair around her face—no docent to yell at him that time. He whispered back but didn't tell me what he said. Oh, her kitchen! Painted the colors of the sun, vines, and sea, filled with pans which warmed tortillas and pots for the best pozole. On the wall, broken pottery, plates smashed and thrown, spelled their names: Frida, Diego. I misremembered. They were simply stones, stones one would gather to skip across water. Large winding trees cooled the courtyard.

Lost among cacti,
I followed your loud laughter.
Hard rain on red clay.

7. Basilica of Our Lady of Guadalupe

I want to do it for my mother,
  Rubi said.
We found an empty aisle and joined   *O Mary, Mother of Names,*
  the service.
Unchurched, unbaptized, polite,
  I tried following
along but fell back with Marcelo.   *the many*
  JD, in the row behind us,
never stood, unmoved
  by a God who's done many no good. *hemmed to your*
                starry cloak,

It's the order I adored:
  listening to the call-   *how many shine*
and-response, watching Rubi,
  one sea rose among many,   *still?*
rise and kneel, pray and speak
  to old rhythms
washing over us. Even those of us   *O Mary, Mother of Leaving*
  seated, unable to speak,
were offered a hand, a few words of greeting. *Roses in Your Wake—*
  I was a stranger,
and they welcomed me. A man crawled   *O Mary,*

  on his knees
toward the Virgin's image.   *Mother of America,*
  He must have worn
his joints and flesh for a while,
  supported by a sister   *I pray for peace of mind.*
or friend. I'd only ever seen
  this in paintings
or documentaries.
  Watching him,

I recalled statues we saw
     climbing to the original church: *American soil*
indigenous men, women, children
     offering all   *will one day claim me,*
they have—cloth, fruit,
     freedom—to the Virgin.   *hopefully,*
The man's pilgrimage
     was not finished
when Rubi told us it's time to go.   *not before my time.*

8. Chapulines at Las Tlayudas

Spritzed with lime

they were still bland
                    but Rubi and I ate them
after a reading
We'd been sipping little pots of mezcal for hours

Rubi stopped eating   grasshopper
          parts on our plate
Pinky up I raised my drink as if
          queen of some realm *Here's to the world*
                    and all its garish colors
                              and the sun-stung agave
may it never run out

You got a little leg in your teeth Rubi said

9. Ballet Folklorico

Sitting next to Marcelo
was almost unnerving.
Excited, his body
was a drum's vibrating skin.

The audience cheered
when the dancers
twirled their bright,
scalloped skirts
in the aisles and some

wearing large, startling
papier-mâché heads
danced near me
like family I had forgotten

because I had forgotten how
profoundly loved
I have been. Lost
in confetti and streamers,
I speak our names

though no one hears.
It was as if we were all dancing.

Epithalamium

Tampa, FL

By now the rain must have stopped
rustling fronds, flowers, and live oak leaves,
the thunder quit its clattering across the sky.
By now the gulls abandon their eaves.
By now students, free from books,
gather on wet porches to debate the big issues
over shiraz. By now fashionable women
wander Hyde Park's jade avenues
for no reason other than their own pleasure.
By now sun-dazzled cars shimmer like champagne.
Together, in the state with the prettiest name,
the state where we are and always wish to be,
older than the others by far, its soil cool,
mutable, and dark as patience or wisdom,
the state into which we welcome
bride and groom, not only him and her, also you,
coming together like rivers whose course
need not be written. Cast your names
into the boundless Gulf—the tide, your refrain—
ever racing, ever run, renewing and renewed.

for Mikey and Lexi

The Marina

        For years I wanted a veil
the color of gulls
        brightening this acre of sky,
veil as in shield and haven, as in
        service to a lord who, without harm,

        entrusts his hand to me, allows my
intimacies and silence. I could be
        unsure without confession. There is a sound
within the sea—neither male nor female—
        that could be the sound

        of my deep-aqua sway.
The wedding party returns.
        Boats and gulls come close to me.
Someone says, *This is heaven.*
        And it can be. What do we know?

        I soak my feet and minnows shine,
exquisite beading
        on the hem of a garment that touches the world;
how desperately
        we consume the water and enter

        the water wishing to be consumed and
nothing changes.
        A black couple camps on a pier—
bubble and rush, flirt and withdraw—
        kissing, stroking their arms,

      dissolving what they perceive
into biography and flesh and dream.
      The younger man leans into the space between
his lover's neck and shoulder and—
      hear the sermon of that old nihilist, the sea?—

they crane their heads and look toward the sun.

Cumberland Island

It was the Spanish or
                          English who brought horses
when this land was conquered and called Florida,
                          their descendants
still gallop on this Georgia coast and lean their muzzles into cordgrass.
                          How many generations does it take
to become feral, to no longer be broken in?
Shining trunks, waist-high grasses, light
                    knotting mossy limbs. Resin on your fingers and salt
                          on mine.
Looking at this guidebook's sepia wildlife photos,
you'd never know anyone lived here before the horses.
                          The Mocama didn't find them useful.
Lapping puddles under slash pines, the horses jolt, moving me
toward a joy I did not give myself

                          room to consider,
trying my damnedest to live

                          in this vulgar country
bracketed by water—

Knight of Cups

minor arcana

—Jump into bed, laughing,
        my longshanks. Forget the ginkgo trees
and waiting for the hour

        their leaves fall in a heap.
Having ridden you,
        let the gold land where it may.

It's not so much my days blur or I can't remember certain
passages of time: you know how birds
mass on the ground, seething instinct and hunger, then

a sound, a scattering—black wing, black wing, black wing—
each with its own particular dark? It's like that in a way.
I used to think one kind of intimacy was the only heal-all.
Can you see what grows along the lake? Moonlight

through haze, through water, through the dark—

Sweeping the floor, I still feel the sweet hum
from before you left, the morning
we drifted from bed to the shower to the kitchen
and back again to watch Joanna Hogg
or Jane Campion, and it wasn't the sex exactly
but its ordinary dailiness, I loved.
We came or we didn't, nothing changed. What a marvel

to share my body, comfortable in it,
with you, my rushlight, who did not hurt me.
I lean the broom near a vase of white peonies.
Apricot jam. Less warm now, the bread.

Exegesis as Self-Elegy

Mark 14:51-52

Remember the boy watching soldiers enter a garden

> (Before the bullets, before I bled out
> on the concrete under an American
>   sun, I loved white roses.)

where the mind cannot imagine more

> (There's a snowbank
> of roses on the sidewalk
>   where America unmade me.)

than what it sees and flesh is transfigured

> (We cannot say this
>   is not an old story.)

and made guilty by bonds alone,

> (The state is always afraid.)

where the disciples mourned and the boy was loved,

> (An education may begin
> with the scent of olive trees
> or busted Heineken bottles
>   greening the air.)

where he scorched the night with his blackness and lived.

Black Magdalene

In one version of her story,
she left Jerusalem for France

by boat, crossing a patrolled sea.
In France, she contemplated.

She dreamed not of Christ but Her
Ladies. Her Ladies sang. Her Ladies

incised wax tablets. Her Ladies revealed
the length of the gown of God.

She saw Her Ladies in trees,
black women climbing or reclining

on branches, like small, silver blossoms,
and knew them in her heart.

January 2017

You are the safest child in the world,
I say to plastic Jesus in the nativity.

My Facebook timeline is a villanelle
of suffering: the boy from Aleppo

whose dust-skin is the color of water
pouring, still, from faucets in Flint.

Drunk, recovering from last year,
my eyes are wet moonflowers.

Christmastide is over. No carolers
approach the well-lit houses.

No one knocks on a stranger's door.
And who would admit them?

Blue Core

Being chased by a white man
on the second floor of Sears
is my earliest memory of panic.

I was the age a kid could get lost
in a rack of clothes. Kids
got lost all the time in the 90s.

Back then, the neighbor's son
taught me to sip honeysuckles.
We were inseparable until he moved.

Where my childhood home should be
there's now a lot, which isn't notable.
Homes flood. Homes packed

with chemicals leveled into the dirt.
The blizzard of '97 left a mountain at the park.
We crawled through a hole at its base

and laughed inside the blue core.
Collecting snow, our multicolored sleds
looked like clothes by a ditch.

The Lost Woods as Elegy for Black Childhood

There used to be no one here,
where cypresses and oaks play
shadow puppets on sawgrass.

You heard the music before
I did: tambourines, pan pipes.
Remember how I woke clean

to meet you each morning?
The dew and the dust?
Remember how you'd catch me

as I fell from trees? Someone
heard and hurt us. I'm Black-Eyed
Pea. You're just Skull Kid.

We wanted our genius to last.
We never wanted chalkboards
or snow. We never came home

before the streetlights buzzed.
All we do is dance in leaves.
Cackle and Dreaming, we call it.

Our mothers call it grief.

Poem for Julián

You look so much like your mother.
You look so much like her by now

you may be tired of hearing it.
May you never be tired of the inexhaustible metaphor

between you and your mother.
In this season of weddings and peach blossoms,

my third grandparent has died.
Being in the world, loss is first and least and awe.

I'm not wise and rarely take advice. I wish I could
end this with *Don't despair* and *Our friends conspire to save our lives.*

I'm sorry for blood on sidewalk chalk. Sorry
for a future I cannot see. A future with hope.

"And Also with You"

for Lauren

I follow your lead: rise when you rise, open
        the hymnal, watch when the priest

smudges your forehead with ashes.
        It's a day you love, your heart setting out

into thickets of restraint. When we turn
        to our neighbors and hold their hands—

dry, cool, or frail—I'm shocked by the casual
        intimacy, drawing me out of the earth,

this thawing earth, where I spent all winter
        weeping, weeping, weeping.

Our Uber takes us back to town while I look
        out the window in my distracted way.

Before opening the door, I kiss your warm cheek.
        You ask where we'll have gimlets later.

Object Label

Derrick Austin (Black, b. 1989)

Crashing the Fête Galante, from the series ***Queer Beatitudes***, 2018
Mixed media on wood panel, with house music

The sky's always pink in the latter days of the empire. Vanessa and
Rubi point their kids toward water birds breaking funny poses to
fly. From Bruno's hammock follow the curve up the berry-blotted
hill where Lauren and the artist share a thermos of tea. Where Suzi
rests, decked out like Moira Rose, the brushwork loosens. Cody's in
the cut eating apples with Alysia. Marcelo blurs down the hill toward
bulrushes on a lake. "Our joy breaks the border between canvas and
frame," Derrick says. "Marcelo bruising his toe. Our scrambling for
ice in the sun."

Taking My Father and Brother to the Frick

Disembark the Turners seem to say,
those starburst barges glowing in the dusk,
but I can't read old Rembrandt,
his guarded eyes are jewels, like black men.
Even the loaned, marble busts
of kings and soldiers fail to arrest you.
It's nearly closing time. The elderly linger,
rapt. Who has looked at either of you lately
with such tenderness?
                              Entering the narrow hall,
I ignore my favorite portraits, their ruffles
and bodices, carnations and powder puffs,
afraid to share my joy with you,
yet your bearing in this space—the procession
of your shoulders, the crowns of your heads—
makes them sing anew.
                              You are both good men.
Walk into the Fragonard Room. You both seem bored still.
It's fine. Perhaps we can progress like these panels,
slowly and without words, here—the city
where I first knew men in the dark—
in this gold and feminine room.

Lilting

In bed, we are lavender together.
We watch the little theater of hours.

Walking her dogs, our neighbor
Crosses the lakeside corner,

Hoop earrings
Echoing the birch's colors.

Tend your joy, you whisper,
As if a charm against eviction or some harm

We might inflict on each other.
For once, I don't hear you

From the room called
Memory. Open the window.

Risk, breath, our seasons,
Let them in. Let them in.

Notes

"Tenderness" borrows language from Emily Brontë's *Wuthering Heights* and Sade's "Sweetest Taboo."

"Is This or Is This True as Happiness" owes its title to a line from George Oppen's "A Theological Definition."

Dorian Corey was a black transwoman and drag queen best known as one of the figures profiled in Jennie Livingston's 1991 documentary *Paris Is Burning*. After Corey passed, the queens of NYC descended on her apartment to claim her jewels and costumes, and a man's mummified remains were discovered. She had killed a robber who broke into her apartment and hid the body in a trunk. Venus Xtravaganza was a transwoman also featured in *Paris Is Burning*. She was murdered before the film's completion.

"My Education" is an obverse, a form invented by Nicole Sealey. The poem's second half is written in reverse order of the first, and the final line is the "thesis question" of the poem.

"Thinking of Romanticism, Thinking of Drake" references the Villa Diodati where Lord Byron, his associate Dr. Polidori, Percy Bysshe Shelley, and Mary Shelley vacationed during the summer of 1816. Byron challenged everyone to write a ghost story. Mary Shelley won the friendly competition with her first novel *Frankenstein*.

"Hotline Bling (Voicemail)" borrows language from Morgan Parker's essay "How to Stay Sane While Black."

George Villiers, 1st Duke of Buckingham, was a favorite of King James I of England and likely his lover.

A jarocho is a dance and style of music from Veracruz with African, Mexican, and Indigenous influences.

"The Lost Woods as Elegy for Black Childhood": In *The Legend of Zelda: Ocarina of Time,* The Lost Woods is a maze-like level full of music that transformed children who wandered inside into monsters known as Skull Kids, playful trickster figures.

Acknowledgments

Many thanks to the editors of the following publications and anthologies where these poems first appeared (sometimes in different form):

Academy of American Poets Poem-A-Day: "The Lost Woods as Elegy for Black Childhood," "Taking My Father and Brother to the Frick";
The Adroit Journal: "Son Jarocho";
Bear Review: "Object Label";
Blood Orange Review: "Sadness Isn't the Only Muse";
BOAAT: "The Witching Hour";
Cherry Tree: "Hotline Bling (Voice Mail)," "Thinking of Romanticism, Thinking of Drake," "January 2017";
The Cortland Review: "Let Them Be Not What They Were Made For," "Lilting," "Little Epic," "Epithalamium" ("By now the rain must have stopped");
Cosmonauts Avenue: "Days of 2014";
Dreginald: "Dorian Corey";
Fantastic Floridas: "Knight of Cups";
Foundry: "'And Also with You'";
fourteen poems: "Blue Core";
Gulf Coast: "Exegesis as Self-Elegy";
HEArt Online: "Letter to Cody on Walpurgisnacht";
Hesperios: "Black Magdalene";
Hobart: "Letter to Brandon," "Poem for Julián";
Image: A Journal of Arts and Religion: "Cachet & Compassion";
Nat.Brut: "Birth Chart," "The Marina";
The Nation: "Tenderness";
The Offing: "Twitter Break: I Watch a Movie";
New England Review: "Dear & Decorations";
Nimrod: "Epithalamium" ("Today I'm happy by myself");
Pleiades: "Black Docent";
Puerto Del Sol: "Late Summer";

The Rumpus: "Proverb," "Black Dandy";
Shade Journal: "To Friendship" (as "The Beginning of Happiness");
The Shallow Ends: "My Education";
Southeast Review: "The Devil's Book," "Remembering God After Three Years of Depression";
Tin House: "Is This or Is This True as Happiness";
underbelly: "Villiers";
wildness: "Cumberland Island";
The Yale Review: "Flies."

"Days of 2014" was translated into Spanish by Marcelo Hernandez Castillo and republished in *Mexico City Lit.*

"The Lost Woods as Elegy for Black Childhood" was reprinted in *Nepantla: An Anthology Dedicated to Queer Poets of Color* (Nightboat Press).

"Days of 2014" was reprinted in *Cosmonauts Avenue Anthology* (Cosmonauts Avenue).

Sections of "Knight of Cups" appeared in the chapbook *Aquarelles* (Pansy Press), a collaboration with Vladislav Beronja, as "Green," "Spleen," and "Beams."

"Late Summer" was reprinted in *New Poetry from the Midwest* (New American Press).

Many of these poems were first written thanks to the invaluable gifts of time and space from the following institutions: Cave Canem, The Hub City Writers Project, The Wisconsin Institute of Creative Writing, and Stanford University.

To Peter, Ron, Sandy, and all the wonderful folks at BOA, I'm awed by all the fantastic work you do. It's been even more of a joy working together the second time.

Mom, Dad, Chris, I love you.

Endless gratitude to my mentors Audrey Colombe, Erica Dawson, Martha Serpas, and Janet Sylvester. May I always give you your flowers. To my groups at CC retreats 2014 and 2015: everything I learned was possible with these poems started in our workshops.

Thanks to Eavan Boland, Louise Glück, Patrick Phillips, and Paisley Rekdal for your invaluable feedback.

My friends have been some of the most sustaining loves of my life. You keep this anxious wreck going. To Cody, my sister in witchery and shenanigans, let's keep living deliciously. To Lauren, thank you for asking me to say how I feel again and again and giving me the space to say it. To Marcelo, you read all these poems from their first drafts, you've heard me at my absolute worst, I love you.

I've been so blessed to be part of so many writing communities. To my dearest dolls, thank you for hearing these poems, for your brilliant minds and generous hearts, for nights over wine, and for endless fun and foolishness in the DMs: Alysia Sawchyn, Laura Theobald, Stephanie Selander, Mikey Rumore, Nicole Robinson, Rubi Hernandez, Rob Bruno, Suzi F. Garcia, Vanessa Angelica Villareal, Brit Bennett, Chris McCormick, Mairead Small Staid, Rachel Harkai, JD Duval, Lorainne Coulter, Vlad Beronja, Natalie Eilbert, Marcela Fuentes, Sarah Fuchs, Jamel Brinkley, Barrett Swanson, Jean Ho, Jordan Jacks, Dantiel Moniz, Mishka Ligot, Oliver Baez Bendorf, Tiana Clark, Tia Clark, Leila Chatti, Marta Evans, Aria Aber, Chekwube O. Danladi, Emily Shetler, Lucy Tan, Mary Terrier, Kate Wisel, Natasha Oladokun, Brandon Taylor, jayy dodd, Victor Xavier Zarour, Phillip B. Williams, Jim Whiteside, Safia Elhillo, Hieu Minh Nguyen, Claire Meuschke, sam sax, Jay Deshpande, Colby Cotton, Monica Sok, Taneum Bambrick, Shangyang Fang, Keith S. Wilson, Callie Siskel, and Paul Tran.

About the Author

Derrick Austin is the author of *Trouble the Water* (BOA Editions, 2016), selected by Mary Syzbist for the A. Poulin Jr. Poetry Prize. His debut collection was honored as a finalist for the 2017 Kate Tufts Discovery Award, the 2017 Thom Gunn Award for Gay Poetry, the 2017 Lambda Literary Award for Gay Poetry, and the 2017 Norma Faber First Book Award.

BOA Editions, Ltd. American Poets Continuum Series

Colophon

The Isabella Gardner Poetry Award is given biennially to a poet in mid-career with a new book of exceptional merit. Poet, actress, and associate editor of *Poetry* magazine, Isabella Gardner (1915–1981) published five celebrated collections of poetry, was three times nominated for the National Book Award, and was the first recipient of the New York State Walt Whitman Citation of Merit for Poetry. She championed the work of young and gifted poets, helping many of them to find publication.

The publication of this book is made possible, in part,
by the support of the following individuals:

Anonymous (x2)
Anya Backlund, Blue Flower Arts
Nelson Adrian Blish
Angela Bonazinga & Catherine Lewis
Elizabeth Forbes & Romolo Celli
Charles & Danielle Coté
The Chris Dahl & Ruth Rowse Charitable Fund
Bonnie Garner
Margaret Heminway
Kathleen C. Holcombe
Nora A. Jones
Paul LaFerriere & Dorrie Parini
Jack & Gail Langerak
The LGBT+ Fund of Greater Rochester
John & Barbara Lovenheim
Joe McElveney
Daniel M. Meyers, *in honor of J. Shepard Skiff*
Sherry Phillips & Richard Margolis Donor Advised Fund
Boo Poulin
Deborah Ronnen
Thomas Smith & Louise Spinelli
Elizabeth Spenst
William Waddell & Linda Rubel